Praise for M. L. Buchman

One of our favorite authors.

Buchman has catapulted his way to the top tier of my favorite authors.

A favorite author of mine. I'll read anything that carries his name, no questions asked. Meet your new favorite author!

M.L. Buchman is guaranteed to get me lost in a good story.

I love Buchman's writing. His vivid descriptions bring everything to life in an unforgettable way.

CHARACTER VOICE

Creating Unique and Memorable Characters

M. L. BUCHMAN

Buchman Bookworks

Sign up for M. L. Buchman's
newsletter today

and receive:
Release News
Free Short Stories
a Free book

Get your free book today. Do it now.
free-book.mlbuchman.com

Other works by M. L. Buchman:

Short Story Series by M. L. Buchman:

The Night Stalkers
The Night Stalkers
The Night Stalkers 5E
The Night Stalkers CSAR
The Night Stalkers Wedding Stories

Firehawks
The Firehawks Lookouts
The Firehawks Hotshots
The Firebirds

Delta Force
Delta Force Short Stories

US Coast Guard
US Coast Guard

White House Protection Force
White House Protection Force Short Stories

Where Dreams
Where Dreams Short Stories

Eagle Cove
Eagle Cove Short Story

Henderson's Ranch
Henderson's Ranch Short Stories

Dead Chef Thrillers
Dead Chef Short Stories

Deities Anonymous
Deities Anonymouse Short Stories

SF/F Titles
The Future Night Stalkers
Single Titles

Contents

In the Beginning

IN THE BEGINNING was the character.

I'm not trying to be sacrilegious at all. I'm talking about story. And I don't care if your story is a romance, a thriller, or science fiction—*character* is the holy grail of story. Yes, even in personal memoir you are developing a character that is more (or sometimes less) like you. But even if it is the truest self you can write, it is still a character you are portraying upon the written page.

Side Note: Science Fiction

Some will argue that science fiction is setting first. Yes, without amazing settings, science fiction fails to entice. But without grab-you-by-the-throat characters, it's never going to rise above the genre. Think about: The Terminator *without* The Terminator *or* Terminator II *without Sarah Connor stepping to the fore,* Alien *without Ripley,* Avatar *without Neytiri, or* The Martian *without Mark Watney having to "science the shit out of this." Not so much.*

Character trumps everything else in story. There are literary books where that masterful character is a dog, cat, or even a city. The movie of 2001: A Space Odyssey *was barely rescued from being just another 1960s psychedelic drug experience by the character of HAL—the ultimate all-powerful computer with the evil eye, a childlike innocence, and a terrifyingly dead-flat monotone.*

The exact same logic can be applied to the plot in a thriller, the puzzle in a mystery, and so on. A powerful character is what lifts the story above the common morass.

Now character voice is by no means the sole element of a great story or series. In his amazing book *Writing the Blockbuster Novel*, Albert Zuckerman identified seven elements that he felt were essential to a truly major novel. His list is:

- High stakes for the character
- Larger-than-life characters
- Powerful dramatic question
- High concept
- Multiple Points of View or POVs (almost always)
- Setting
- Family

The first two and the last are firmly anchored in character (in fact they all are, but to understand that, I recommend reading his book). For the purposes of this book, all we need to know at this moment is that character is screamingly important and making that character distinct must be one of our primary duties as a writer.

Voice

Digging a little deeper for a moment, I want to define Character Voice. It isn't just how a character speaks.

It's how they:

- Speak
- Respond
- Think
- Act
- React
- Fight
- Make love
- …and everything else.

It's how they move and look as well.

Let me repeat that again: a character's looks are part of what I define as the character's overall voice. Voice, in the way I think of it and mean it in this book, is the character's complete presentation upon the page (or stage or screen).

All of these are shaped by their past, present, and hoped-for future. It can change based on their physicality or their family. Did they serve in a military unit, work at a law firm, ride a horse, or sail single-handed around the world? Are they white, Latino, from a small Pacific Island, quadriplegic, or deathly allergic to nuts? Are they five-foot-nothing tall but couldn't give a damn or six-four and incredibly self-conscious of it? Every one of these elements will shape and alter that overall voice.

Character Voice is the embodiment of everything we know about a character. Delving deeper into this is what this book is about.

Sounds Like Me

The challenge for a writer is to develop characters that don't sound just like you (except in memoir…perhaps).

Why? Isn't that the "writer's voice" that we've heard so much about?

No.

(Hope that's clear enough.)

Not even a little!

('Nuff said?)

The writer's voice is something that you can't help. It's part of who you are. Are you a meticulous grammarian, a natural joker, someone who loves a neat turn of phrase? Are metaphors a key tool in your trade? Or thriller pacing? Dark versus light? Sweet versus gritty? Techno versus ethereal?

Those are all parts of *your* voice.

Reread the first several lines of this section. Is that the way you would have written something even that straight-forward? Not likely. That's my voice. It may shift and vary depending on fiction vs. nonfiction, genre, or even the amount of tension at a moment in a story, but all that is the writer's voice. My writer's voice is already distinct. I can hone it—perhaps (and that's a big perhaps)—by not messing with it. The more I can leave it alone, the more likely it is to be my true writer's voice. Weird, but true (and not the subject of this book, so I'm dropping that here). I just wanted to be clear what I *wasn't* talking about.

What I learned as I wrote more and more stories was that I had to learn to make my *characters'* voices distinct. If I didn't, then they *did* all sound like me—meaning they all sounded the same. Not a good thing in a four-hundred-page, multiple-POV novel. My writer's voice still comes through loud and clear, but it must be expressed through unique, engaging characters.

The various characters still share my writer's voice. They still are created from my worldview. Their thoughts and actions may be narrated much more in my natural voice than their dialog is. But even there, they must think, act, speak, move, etc. in their own voices.

Imagine a whole series in which the characters are indistinguishable.

Oh, wait, you don't have to imagine it, you've probably read them. Or started to. The next time you just "set aside" a book (especially Book 2 or 3 in a series) and aren't really sure why, think about it. The chances are it's because all of the characters sounded the same. The setting may sound fresh, but the characters don't and that is what ultimately holds us in a book.

Side Note: The Singular Amazing Character

Has Lee Child held you for twenty-four (so far) Jack Reacher tales? Some people, absolutely. He has created a masterful character: the true outsider who keeps revealing his heart of gold despite his best efforts to the contrary.

Did Mr. Child keep you involved for even five or ten titles about the same person? If so, he did that by slowly evolving the character, and how much we secretly wish we could be like him: strong enough to play outside the rules.

If he lost you along the way? It's probably because at the end of the day, it's still Jack Reacher the loner.

Is this a trap or a key to success? You'll have to decide for yourself. Mr. Child sells vastly more books than I do. But I also know that, despite my love for a good thriller, I personally stopped regularly reading his books a while ago.

I can hear a common answer to differentiating characters, because I used to think this way too: *But I dressed them
differently and gave them different looks.*

Yes, we'll talk about that. It *can* be a very effective tool
in shaping character voice, but it is just one of many in
what makes a character's voice unique. And it's one of the
lesser ones for most characters. I've read series where that
is the *only* differentiation and it became so tedious that I
stopped twenty pages into Book Three: "Oh no, not that
same voice—again."

Series Thinking

This problem is significantly compounded in a series.
Characters who we meet casually in Book One must be
wholly distinguishable from the foreground characters.
They also must be consistent in later books. This is especially true in romances or any team-based series where a
former minor character may become the predominant
character in Book Four or Fourteen.

Imagine a circle of four women friends (the basis of
two of my series I'll be using as examples later). Each character must be so distinctive that when it is time for Perrin's
book, the reader can't wait to read that book. Why?
Because Perrin's voice is so unique and powerful that the
reader had been looking forward through the series to
reading that one, unique character's story. And then
Melanie's after that.

Not all distinctivenesses (there's a word for you) are
created equal. No matter how carefully we plan, some
characters just *pop!* I'll talk later about the arrangement of
a series and my thoughts on the best way to order one of
those voices in a series.

Hint: think about it hard before putting the strongest first.

Practice

This book is all about tools. Tools I've tried and tools I'm planning to try. Tools from classes gone by and tools that I've adapted to my own needs.

But here I have to say a word about practice.

My friend Dean Wesley Smith says that he thinks of writing a book as the best practice for writing the next book after that—he's the epitome of a long-term career thinker (as he should be after almost forty years as a full-time writer). So he chooses one skill he wants to practice with each title and focuses on enhancing that skill *and only that skill.*

Why do I bring that up here?

I'm going to be discussing a lot of different tools in this book. Do *not* try to do them all at once. All you'll end up with is brain lock before you can write or gobbledygook once you've written. And those are the best scenario results.

This bears repeating: *Do not try using all these tools at once!*

As you work with one tool, especially for the length of an entire book, it will slowly become implanted in your writer's toolbox.

Side Note: Toolbox

Stephen King has a great discussion on this toolbox in his book On Writing. *Therefore I'll direct you there except to say that this book is a set of tools I've used for character voice. All of which, to varying degrees, are now in my toolbox. Some are favorites, worn to familiarity with long use, some I reach for only on special occasions, and some were tried, then dropped into a corner and forgotten. Part of the reason I'm writing this book is to dig into that toolbox and rediscover tools that were too unfamiliar or perhaps even too advanced when I first tried them.*

By practicing one tool, you take ownership of it and can use it more effectively. You will eventually train it into your subconscious and it will simply come out the next time you need it. Meanwhile, you'll be practicing the next tool. A writer's career is rarely about leaps and bounds. It is about incremental improvement.

Dan Brown has stated in interviews that *The Da Vinci Code* was supposed to just be the next book in a budding midlist career. Instead it broke out and remained on the *New York Times* Best Sellers list for 136 weeks. In the publishing industry it is simply called a phenomenon. No one—including his publishers—expected anything exceptional from that title. It simply broke out.

But if you go back and read his prior three books, you can see him practicing a structural and pacing element until he had it honed. (And he spent a lot of time working on other skills and developing Robert Langdon in *Angels & Demons.*) Whether the practicing was conscious or not, I don't know. But it seemed clear to me when I read the books in the order they were written (*Digital Fortress, Angels & Demons, Deception Point,* then *The Da Vinci Code*). It is but one of the many reasons for the book's popularity, but that it was incremental practice seems obvious to me.

J. K. Rowling did much the same through the Harry Potter series. You can see her learning to write, book by book. She began with amazing characters in an amazing world and a decent level of craft. Then continually practiced her craft as she told the next six stories. But for this reader, her great success was because she never for an instant lost sight of her characters. Whether it was conscious or not on her part, by the end of this book you'll have a good idea of how she might have made three such distinct and memorable characters as Harry, Ron, and Hermione.

No. Practicing the tools in this book, or any book, doesn't guarantee that you'll be the next King or Rowling. (I wish.) But *not* practicing them will guarantee that you won't become one.

Avoiding Overwhelm

Again: Do *not*, I repeat, *not* try to use all of these tools at once. Your head exploding would be the least of your problems. You can create a very effective writer's block this way. Or, if you can write, you'll be so far in your head that what you write will be utter and total crap.

Personally, I'd rather sign up for my head exploding out of those three options.

I choose one thing to practice at a time. And I don't get very compulsive about it. I might approach a novel with a thought like one of these:

- I'm going to think more about how we interact with our clothes as I write this story. (I may achieve this by simply making a character who really cares about clothes as I did with my fashion designer in my Where Dreams series.)
- I'm going to work on describing the qualities of nighttime outdoors. (A common theme for my Night Stalkers warriors—they're called that because they fly most of their missions in darkness.)
- I'm going to really focus on how family

influences who we are. (I might do this by making the hero's and heroine's backgrounds so drastically different that it becomes a central issue for them. I do this a lot, but *Wait Until Dark* (Night Stalkers #3) is a particularly good example from my own work. She is an Army orphan—her parents both died in the service by the time she was twelve. Yet her love interest was all about a big, close family who are totally involved in each other's lives.)

The result of these challenges and myriad others that I've done is a way to practice without, consciously, practicing. This way my editing brain doesn't interfere with my creative brain, but I'm still learning an essential skill.

One last example to show that you can practice very technical craft skills without getting some editing side of your brain in the way.

I wanted to learn about cliffhangers. I wanted to really get good at how I put the hook at the end of one scene to force the reader into the next. This is how the top writers keep you awake way late into the night because you can't put their book down. They and their craft *won't let you!*

So here's what I did:

- First I pulled out a half dozen books that I could never put down, not when reading them, not when rereading them. The list looked something like this: *Born in Fire* by Nora Roberts, *The Da Vinci Code* by Dan Brown, *Jack & Jill* by James Patterson, *The Hard Way* by Lee Child, and a few others. (You can tell I did this almost ten years ago.)
- I then opened up my standard manuscript

format and typed in the last sentence of every chapter and the first one of the next, through all of the books. This let me study, in a very visceral way, how these different authors who were the masters of their craft used cliffhangers.

- I then closed all those books, closed the file, and tried not to think about what I had learned.
- I then chose a story that *required* good cliffhangers to work. It included two timelines. Timeline One: my characters meet and slowly fall in love in a romance that, due to circumstances and personalities, takes years. Timeline Two: my characters have to draw on the story of their courtship years to survive a crisis twenty years after they were finally married. So one timeline is under twenty-four hours of the present, the other spans at least five years of the past.
- I placed the two timelines in alternating chapters. This created the challenge of how to keep the reader from skipping chapters to read all of one timeline or all of the other.
- The end of every chapter therefore had to have a double cliffhanger. One hooked you forward to stay interested in the timeline you were reading. The other hooked you into the timeline you weren't reading. And the opening of every chapter had the same two hooks: one to pick up from the earlier chapter in that timeline and one to pick up from the immediately preceding chapter in the other timeline.

- This book, *Frank's Independence Day*, went on to be one of my bestselling titles.

I included this whole explanation not to convince you to practice cliffhangers in this exact way (though it wouldn't hurt) or to buy my book (though I wouldn't complain). I did it to show how practicing that tool—a very complex one—can be done without interfering with your creative process, whatever that may be.

The tools in *this* book can be practiced in exactly the same way.

The Shoe That Fits

All I offer here is a set of tools.

Try them on for size.

If one doesn't fit, cast it aside and try another.

Some of these tools worked for me for a time, but then I outgrew them. Is it because of a lack of utility in that tool? No. It's because I found another tool that worked better for me, that pushed me in a new direction. I don't expect my current tool set to last either. It's always changing and shifting as my skills grow and my interests shift.

Other of these tools are ones I'm only beginning to test for a good fit.

Many of these tools, including the ones I use currently, I mostly became aware of using after the fact. I would finish a book and realize that I had done something new. I'd even set out to practice one thing and end up learning another.

In preparing the presentation on which this book is based, I began going over the notes that accumulate around any work in progress. As I did so, I began to see that there was a method to my madness (at least on occasion), and that with some effort, I could turn these into coherent tools.

There's a great divide in writing that is worth mentioning when we're talking about tools and personal writing styles: Plotter versus Pantser. The first type of writer pre-plans everything and the other writes by the seat of their pants.

Some see it as the great divide between high heels and hiking boots and never the twain shall meet. I've written entire books starting with no more than a name, a setting, and a first sentence (and been accused of not being a true pantser because I already knew too much). I've written entire books based on an outline that covered floor-to-ceiling whiteboards (and been told that wasn't "real" outlining).

Folks, get over it. It's a continuum. There are also flats, sneakers, runners, cowboy boots, oxfords, wingtips, Birkenstocks, and everything else mixed in between. But that's not my real point (a drawback of analogies is that they want to run away with me). In my opinion, a plotter is someone who simply does their first draft (or "discovery draft") in an outline format.

Twice I've had the pleasure of hearing Terry Brooks talk about writing his immensely successful Shannara series.

After the first talk, we had a great chat about our preferred outlining tools. We had both recently discovered ECCO as an upgrade from Grandview and WordPerfect before that... (yes, I'm dating myself). But we had a great time trading tips on favorite features. I used ECCO to track notes, but Terry's final outlines were so in-depth in ECCO that he said they were nearly entry-per-sentence and all he had to do was turn them into English line by line and he was done. He did *all* of his drafts except the final one in the outliner.

At the second talk a couple years later, I was assisting at the conference. He gave much the same outlining speech to the crowded room of eight hundred writers. Afterward, we sat down to chat for a bit and I asked if he really still used ECCO (I had long since left true outlining behind and moved on to mind-mapping on whiteboards).

Quick Side Note: Not About Software

This is not a book about software tools. Scrivener, ECCO (the modern version), Org-Mode, OneNote, or any of that. This is about conceptual tools. (Just in case you were looking for the Scrivener chapter, there isn't one.)

Terry glanced around to make sure we were alone. "Still outline? Are you kidding me? I just write the damn thing. But that's a room of mostly beginners and I had to give them a tool that they could use. They need a process so they have a chance of finishing that first novel, and it *will* work for them now as well as it worked for me then." I also learned from him that day about tuning your talk to your audience.

Process

From the example of those two talks with Terry Brooks, please take away that plotter vs. pantser is just a tool, nothing more—just like the tools I'll be discussing here. Also, the tools that work best for you may change with time. Remember to be flexible.

The tools here can be used to help develop characters in a book or a series. They can also be used after the first draft is written to understand what was created and what is waiting to be fixed in the second draft. My use of my present tools is more a design-as-I-build plan.

My current process looks something like this (If your process is different, and I expect that it is, it doesn't mean that it's wrong. It means that it's yours.):

- I do some brainstorming about what the next book will be: world, setting, character.
- I think about what *one* technique I'd like to work on next as a writer. (It might not be about character voice. It could be about setting, pacing, family, or any challenge you face.)
- I start writing.
- I do some more writing.
- Partway into the story I start to learn more of who the characters are and how they sound. I'll often backtrack to the beginning at this time to incorporate what I've learned about those characters' voices.
- At some point, I get stuck. This can happen for a ton of reasons, one of which is character.
- I try a couple of other tools, even old ones I typically no longer use, to try and figure out why I'm stuck.
- When I'm done with the first draft (vast simplification there), I finally (*finally!*) can clearly hear my characters' true voices. So, my very first note on every second-draft to-do list is "Fix voices." (My second is always, "Deepen setting"—an entirely different topic outside the scope of this book.) I "fix voices" because otherwise the way I wrote their voices in the beginning won't match what I wrote by the end.

This is especially true for the first book in a series or a stand-alone title.

- In the second draft, I "tune them up," repairing any faults or lacks in their voices. (Note: I don't rewrite or do a deep edit, I fix and move on.)

This will make more sense once you've read through this book. Though I've also used these tools to create detailed series outlines before I wrote a word. But this book is about Character, not about outlining.

So let's leap in.

2

Traditional Tools

THESE ARE some tools that seem to be taught in every writing course on the planet. That's why I call them traditional tools. Sometimes they're very useful, sometimes they are using a jackhammer to staple a piece of paper.

Pros And Cons

These tools, or any tools for that matter, can be helpful or detrimental.

They can provide:

- Consistency – once you know who the character is.
- Continuity – how they grow and change over time.
- Clarity – (or distinctiveness is also a good word) helps make them unique.

They can also:

- Squelch – your imagination might stop because, after all, you already have everything you need in "The Tool."
- Confine – not allowing your character to expand or shift because "The Tool" says they're like *this* even though they seem to be more like *that* as you write them.
- Detract – actually remove your writer's voice from the character. This last one is interesting and insidious. The problem is, when you are using some of these tools, you will be in an editing mindset. You will include what you *think* should be there for that character. It will then inhibit any opportunity for your creative mind, which becomes active when you're writing (or creatively outlining), to expand on that. Why? Because you've managed to disconnect the character from your creative voice (which is the smarter one) and trap them in your editing voice (which can kill good writing faster than a speeding lead brick).
- Become Unwieldy – The Tool can become so large that you actually never use it.

So, again, use any of these tools carefully.

The Character Interview

The character interview seems to be the true classic. I started with a very basic one from the first writing class I ever took. I then expanded it until it was such a monster that…I never used it despite spending hours (days / weeks) completing it. It was incredibly helpful to me as a beginning writer and I do still go back to tiny portions of it on occasion to understand specific things about my character that seem to stump me. Here is (more or less) my final form of this interview questionnaire that I would spend untold hours filling out for every single character.

This example is for my very first book, a fantasy novel entitled *Cookbook from Hell*. A surprising amount of it held true in the writing (almost half). At least until twenty years later when I completely redrafted it and re-released it as *Cookbook from Hell: Reheated*. I think the only thing that survived into that redraft was her friendship with Michelle. Even her name changed by the time I was done.

But as I mentioned, there was a time this was very useful, so I'm including it in some detail here.

- **Name:** Denise Bertolli
- **Nickname:** none
- **Age/bday:** 37 / March 14
- **Sign:** Pisces
- **Sex:** F
- **Looks & clothes:** 5' 2-1/2", 110 lbs., shoulder-length brown hair, med complexion, nice casual clothes (cords, blouses, loafers or low-heels), no jeans, likes to "fancy-up" on occasion.
- **Diction, accent, etc.:** no obvious accent, excellent diction, few contractions, voice high without being squeaky.
- **Education:** Andover High School, MA / BA psych, Amherst / MFA non-fiction writing, Cornell.
- **Vocation(s):** 3 years McGraw-Hill photo services clerk, 4 years NYT lifestyles desk, 2 years lifestyle editor NYT, 2 years editor for East River Press.

- **Status & money:** status not important, friends are. Makes $70kpy +/-, doesn't live extravagantly.
- **Ambitions:** live and grow old somewhere far from New York (maybe AZ, maybe San Juan Islands in WA).
- **Relationship status:** has known John for years, met him at McGraw-Hill when 26. Just started dating seriously at start of book. Engaged by end of book.
- **Sexual history:** started young (15) and a bit wild through college. First serious relationship lasted from 20-27. Nothing over a year since.
- **Family, ethnicity:** mother died in childbirth, dad (Vic) / Aunt Elena & Uncle Joshua raised her.
- **Relationships (work/friends):** very close with boss, Carolyn, and assistant, Julie. Best friends, outside of John's brother (Henry) and 2 cousins (Janet and Mary), are Alan and Patricia who she goes on very outdoorsy, 3-week vacations with every fall. Has only a few other friends at any level.
- **Places (home, office, car...):** lives in rent-controlled artist's loft in a run-down security building just off 14th in Greenwich Village. Apartment interior has been remodeled and is very attractive in a hodgepodge of styles: oriental rugs, Indonesian batiks, & NW Indian wood-carved salmon. Office is mainly in corner of living room, but also has very immaculate space with a view and a single Miro original at East River Press. Never learned to drive.
- **Possessions:** books! And an exquisite kitchen.

- **Recreations, hobbies:** hiking, kayaking, and sailing. All done with the intensity of the type A+ that she is.
- **Obsessions:** has no patience for her own messes, except on vacation and is then an utter slob. Hates suits and the people that wear them with the passion of long experience.
- **Religion & beliefs:** raised sort of, kinda, relaxed Roman Catholic...a bit. Now mild agnostic, wants to believe, just not sure in what.
- **Politics:** just left of center. Believes in capital punishment only for anyone that hurts her friends or family.
- **Superstitions:** knocks on head instead of wood.
- **Fears:** losing control of her environment.
- **Attitudes:** the participant.
- **Character flaws:** a bit thorny around the edges, almost brittle when she's working. No patience with people who move slowly at work.
- **Character strengths:** very creative. Very solution oriented. Always completes everything.
- **Pets:** two cats that she lost along with first serious relationship. New puppy, George.
- **Taste in books, music, food...:** classics, nonfiction (closet mystery hound). If the music postdated Puccini and predated the Beatles, forget it. No country, no rap, no hard rock. Never Elvis under any conditions (Love-interest John loves Elvis; he's allowed one album per week in her presence.) Loves food in any manner, shape, or form, but especially Italian and French.
- **Correspondence:** keeps up correspondence

with college friends as meticulously as everything else she does.

- **Handwriting:** completely illegible. Has written in poor block print since her aunt outlawed her script in 10th grade.
- **Talents:** loves to sing and is always slightly off-key. Has given up more instruments than most people have ever touched.
- **What's in wallet:** one credit card, photo-ID, med card, $50–150, and a list of top fifteen phone numbers in her life. That's it.
- **Sentences of motion/conflict:** Denise lifted her fingers off the keyboard, tilted her head sideways for a moment while scowling at the screen. She slapped "save," punched the main power switch, and then leaned her head down on the keyboard. John started to massage her neck and shoulders. Small groans of pleasure rose from the depths of the keyboard where her head still rested as he found the hard knots under her shoulder blades. "I think I'll keep you," she said.
- **Sentences of childhood:** Denise was six years old the first time she stood out on the point of Little Captain Island. She leaned hard against her father's leg as the summer wind played with her hair. He told her that this was where her mother was, where her ashes had rested for six long years. He told her of the blessings her mother had made for her when she knew childbirth would be her death. He did not tell her of the curses, he chose to bear those himself. The benevolent figure of her mother, not as seen in the photos on the mantlepiece at

home, but as captured by the sea-foam breaking on the rocks where her mother and father had first met, was to be a guidance to her throughout her life. She swore at that moment, with all the sincerity of a six-year-old, to live the life her mother had never had. It wasn't until that night that she finally cried herself to sleep in her father's lap.

- **Sentences of work:** Denise always left a wake behind her wherever she went. All five foot two "and a half" of her breezed into the conference room. The senior editor and three-star reporters stopped their heated debate and looked up. She dropped a stack of copy into the senior editor's lap. / "This is how the copy should read and don't let one of these hacks edit it," she said waving at reporters. She strode out of the room leaving a stunned silence. There was little chatter as the editor at first quickly, then more slowly, read through the copy. / He looked up at the others and said, "Who is she?"

- **Sentences of entering close relatives' home:** Denise walked through the open front door and shed her skin behind her. No worries about appearances, manners, or propriety ever entered her Uncle Joshua's house. Passing through the dining room and the swinging door into the kitchen, she found Aunt Elena and Uncle Joshua consulting over a soup pot. She waved a bottle of wine and managed to say, "I hope you have enough for me, too," before disappearing into one of Uncle Joshua's famous bear hugs as he shouted in joy, the way he always greeted her after even just an hour apart.

- **Sentences when trapped in an empty white room:** Denise has two moods and a blank white room does not invoke her relaxed, calm, playful mood. She stands in the center of the room turning very slowly on her heel as she looks around. She walks twice around the room, once relatively fast and a second time more slowly, pushing and nudging the wall as low and high as she could reach. After pacing the space several times to get its size, she sits down cross-legged in the exact center and scowls at the wall for a long time before thinking of anything at all.

- **Sentences of emotion:** Denise looked at John as if seeing him for the first time, lying back on the beach with his arm over his eyes. Tears began to roll down her cheeks as she saw his real peace and contentment with the world; a peace she had never known. She had been so afraid of being successful and finding that state was empty that she had driven herself very close to being a complete failure. She thought, "I could shed all that garbage and just keep moving. I can pause, take a deep breath, and take a step. It may not be in just the right direction, but if I never give up, I'll get to where I want to go. Where I *want* to go..." / She suddenly realized that John was watching her with a quizzical smile, "What are you smiling at?" / She hadn't realized she was.

- **Sentences of old age:** Denise pushed the starched-stiff sheet away from her neck. John had gone ten years ago; it was finally time to follow him on. She felt a strong hand take hers. Glad her friend was here at the end, she opened her eyes. / "I still don't believe you're the Devil." Her own smile was answered in Michelle's face.

- **Etc.**

It is quite a mouthful, isn't it? But you get the idea. It is one way to get a good handle on a character.

Side Note: Don't Leave a Tool That's Working

While I haven't used the full "Interview" technique since my very early writing, that doesn't mean that you won't either.

Suzanne Brockmann in many ways actually created the military romance subgenre. She has had a massive career to which I can only vaguely aspire. She spends immense effort building 100-200 pages of notes including: outlines, character profiles, research notes, and all the rest of it And she has done it for book after book after book. It still works for her.

If it works for you, don't junk it. Every writer is different.

I do still use selected sections of the Interview, especially when I get stuck. The questions I particularly like and still use on occasion are:

- **Sentences of Motion/Conflict:** I find this to be a particularly effective question. I'll spend a lot of time watching a movie that has a character similar to one I want to write. How do they act, react, and move? Do they touch their fingertips together while thinking of what to say or pop the interrogator in the nose? (I once cast a masseuse's hands for one of my female characters and that became one of her key tells. I was fascinated by the character's hands and they always told the reader about the character's true feelings—that she never revealed in any other way if she could help it.)

- **The White Room:** It helps me discover how the person deals with themselves. One is amused and pulls out a tattered paperback I didn't know she'd smuggled in. Another unearthed a black marker pen and indulged himself in being a bad boy by drawing on the walls despite being a Dudley Do-Right to all appearances. Yet another character set in to worrying first about what he'd done wrong to get stuck in the white room, then how to survive, then who he'd ticked off to get stuck here, then… It tells me a lot about who they are.

- **Sentences of Childhood:** A bit about childhood, background, and family. The more I books I write, the more I use this question.

- **Sentences of Old Age:** It gives me a view back into the story…sometimes. I use it more often when the story is stuck rather than the character. What was the long perspective? What was the emotion when they think back to the time that the story happened?

- **If you have a favorite interview question:** I'd love to hear it. I might even include it in a 2nd edition. Just send it to characters@mlbuchman.com.

The Journal

I've spoken with some writers who write their characters' daily journals. They'll sometimes spend weeks and thousands of words journaling to discover what their character cares about and what their written voice is.

One of the more intriguing comments I heard was from a writer who used the daily character journal as warm-up exercise for writing. It set the voice in her head and allowed her to plunge directly into the story.

I'm not a journaler by nature, but I'd say that anything that gets a writer deeper into the character's voice should be seriously considered. I certainly tried it a number of times before dismissing it.

The Short Story

Some people write a short story about their character that's outside the scope of the novel.

Because I write a lot of romances, this doesn't work well for me. Why? Once I find someone's true love, how am I supposed to find another one for them in a longer work? They've already found their perfect match. Oh, sometimes I squeeze in a wedding story or something, but short story-to-novel doesn't work for me myself as a tool.

The other problem I have (again, this is about knowing yourself as a writer) is that once I've written someone's story, romantic or not, I'm not particularly interested in telling it again even in a longer, more detailed form.

However, there are innumerable examples of doing this successfully including: *The Martian Child* by David Gerrold, which a Nebula and Hugo Award–winning novelette written in 1994 and 1995. It was rewritten as a novel in 2002. And eventually became *Martian Child* the movie in 2007.

My friend Kristine Kathryn Rusch will often write a short story to discover what happens next. Or sometimes it will be set at the same time as something happening in the story, but at a location outside the scope of the novel so that she can understand what is happening over there and how it might affect what's happening over here. As a bonus, she often gets a sellable short story out of the exercise, but that's not why she writes them. She writes them because it is a part of her process.

I'll write a short story about a character but not as a part of developing a novel. It will be:

- A prequel like: *The Heart of the Storm* to find out how two war buddies met five years earlier. I didn't use it in a novel, instead it was just because I wanted to know. As a bonus, my fans did too.
- A sequel like: *Emily's Christmas Gift*, set five years later than the novel to see how she's dealing with retirement from the military.
- Or even a side-quel like: *Dilya's Christmas Challenge*, of an on-going, fan-favorite character, which is a side story to *Emily's Christmas Gift*.

But none of my stories are about direct discovery at the time of initially learning about the character. I've tried it a few times, and I guess it has worked because those bits of exploratory storytelling have ended up in the novels themselves. I suppose that I have simply incorporated that backstory exploration directly into my novel writing process somewhere along the way.

Still, it is a common tool that many writers use very effectively.

Observation by Others

Still stuck? Try writing what your other characters think of that character or how to interact with them. Perhaps even what they sound like? Irritatingly clipped, vociferously impassioned, taciturn, talkaholics, tone like a bell, tone like a disaster siren, sexy-as-hell, soothing, etc.

Side Note: Observation by Others Within a Story

A great tip: How do we know that Denise (of the Character Interview above) is an awesome lady? John loves her, Joshua is proud of her, and the totally jaded Michelle befriends and thoroughly enjoys her companionship.

It is a great discovery tool even if the scene doesn't make it into the finished work. Jump over to someone else's head and see what they think about the character who is giving you trouble. Ask them the hard questions. I'm always surprised what comes to life when I try this one.

3

Diving Inward

OVER THE YEARS I've built a set of tools to distinguish my various characters. It helps me split their voices apart and make them distinct. Sometimes I use this collection of tools more effectively than others, but that isn't the point here.

The thing I find so exciting about this set of techniques is that I haven't begun to plumb their depths even though I've been using these tools for some years now. I'm going to now walk through this tool set in great depth with some built-in examples from my books.

The fact that they're my characters is only because I know them so well and know how I developed them so they make great examples for how this cluster of tools works together. I could have picked other books, but it would be impossible to select a title everyone had read. How well I actually used those tools in my fiction…well, that's not part of this book (personally, I think I rocked it, but hey, that's just me).

Look at the four pictures on the following page. Spend

a moment really looking at them, we're going to be discussing them in some depth.

Four Night Stalker Women

The Supreme Pilot

The Latina Gunner

The Mechanic Next Door

The Wildcard Pilot

Just looking at their faces—never mind their titles—can you even *imagine* them having the same voice?

Nope? Me neither.

But how do we set about distinguishing them?

Side Note: For Fans of My Fiction

These four women (U.S. Navy Lt. Patricia A. Denkler, Michelle Rodriguez, Anna Kendrick, and Zoe Saldana) are rough approximations of how I picture the women in the first four books my series The Night Stalkers. I wrote this series about the first women to, fictionally, join the real-life Night Stalkers helicopter regiment—the US Army's 160th Special Operations Aviation Regiment, or SOAR.

Five Aspects of a Character

In developing these characters, I break them down by five distinct aspects. I make their:

- *Looks* distinct.
- *Childhood/formative* years distinct.
- *Family* distinct.
- *Occupation* distinct.
- *Attitude* distinct.

If I do this, *then* the character *IS* distinct.

I'm going to risk being a little confusing here for a moment. These five aspects will change *how* a character responds internally to the world around them. Later on we'll discuss how the character combines this with other aspects of their personality, which will control how they think and speak to give voice to that response. For now, just tuck away that this is only one aspect of what forms a distinct character.

I'm going to go into some detail about each of these characters. I'm doing this so that you can see how I've used each of these aspects in different ways to develop varied personalities.

Side Note: My Editing Ah-ha Moment

My first draft of my first novel was (shall we be kind) hideous. I gave it to four friends to read. One suggested I hire an editor, another never spoke to me about my writing again though I know that he now reads many of them, and a third told me "This is such shit! Whatever gave you the idea you could write?" (Yeah, really.)

The fourth one gave me the right advice and did so very kindly: "Perhaps you should take a class." I did.

And the day I turned into a writer was during the third class when the instructor said, "You can't edit a novel. You can't edit a chapter. Or even a scene. If you're good you can edit a paragraph, but in the beginning, you're lucky if you can edit a sentence."

I had been trying to edit "my novel" for almost a year without success. But once I realized that it wasn't a single entity and I could take it apart and put it back together, I was finally able to start working on it.

This particular tool set that I'm exploring here is how I develop characters. And it is tied to the concept of understanding the elements of a character separately so that I can then build an interesting and unique character.

Does this work as a pantser? Of course! I've done it that way many times. As I write, I discover their: looks, past, family, occupation, attitudes. I'm just saying that it's useful to be able to think of each of these separately.

Looks

The *Supreme Pilot,* inspired by Lieutenant Denkler. (I'll be referring to them by their labels to save you wanting to go back to their photos, and yes, I will show them all again at the end of the discussion for your convenience.) She definitely has her shit together, just looking at her. Pretty, competent, perhaps reserved. Wearing a flightsuit, she isn't afraid to roll up her sleeves and get to work. She wears designer sunglasses rather than the more stereotypical Ray-Ban mirrored Aviator sunglasses, meaning that she isn't at all afraid to be herself. One of the other characteristics that I discovered about this character was from how she thought about her own looks: she really doesn't give a shit. Guys react to the pretty blonde, but she doesn't care. She's a hundred percent about the flying.

The *Latina Gunner*, inspired by Michelle Rodriguez, looks tough and driven. She wears a low-cut dress or a tight t-shirt because she knows she has a killer body and, if men are willing to be idiots staring at it, she's fine leveraging that to get what she wants. Her tough, "Don't be messing with me" attitude and the skills to back it up combine to make her a force of nature. Extrovert, funny, sexy, and very hard-edged.

The *Mechanic Next Door*, inspired by Anna Kendrick, is just that. She's the wholesome, unremarkable girl next door —who also happens to be smart as hell. If you doubt that, just watch Anna's Oscar-nominated performance in *Up in the Air*. For my story, that brilliance is as a helicopter mechanic (she has an eidetic memory), but it is the girl-next-door looks that makes everyone underestimate this character.

The *Wildcard Pilot*, inspired by Zoe Saldana, has flexibility and range as shown by Zoe's performances in *Avatar, Colombiana,* and the *Star Trek* series among others. Well aware of her beauty and skin color, she doesn't leverage them the way the *Latina Gunner* does. Instead, she uses her sense of humor and slightly wicked smile to hide the person inside.

Then I started to drill a little deeper.

Childhood / Formative Years

The *Supreme Pilot* has a key piece of her personality from this period that is all about her and not about her family.

She grew up with a mad crush on the boy next door. He was six years her senior, but she was incredibly precocious and constantly challenged him. In fact, it became the root cause of the hard-driven determination that was to be at the core of who she was. In trying to keep up with the older boy, she constantly pushed herself to the limits, and does so until she knows no other way to be. She mitigates that hard drive with a narrow sliver of humor that came from teasing him to get his attention (like filling his senior prom–night shoes with grape jelly).

In sharp contrast, the *Latina Gunner* grew up on the streets of East Los Angeles. In many ways, it is no better than a Third World barrio. Gangs, death, sex, and drugs were all around her every day. She learned fast that there was a power to being female, but also a danger. So the *Latina Gunner* turned herself into a badass fighter as well. She's pulled herself up by her own bootstraps and doesn't care who the hell knows that about her. Though her actual past she keeps desperately buried. Going back to looks, she has a small stripe of golden-blonde in her dark hair. It is to remind her of her best friend—a teenage prostitute who died in her arms after a random drive-by shooting. It is a talisman that life is short and it is a battle to the death.

The *Mechanic Next Door* spent most of her childhood alone. The one thing she had access to were Army helicopters because her father was an Army crew chief on a Black Hawk. Orphaned at twelve, she cared for herself and her dying grandmother—her ticket to staying out of foster care. She has learned that no one can help her and that she absolutely stands alone.

The *Wildcard Pilot* was always beautiful and it got her all of the wrong kind of attention. Rather than confronting it head-on, or using it like the *Latina Gunner*, it pushed her around. Avoiding her single father's friends and their roving hands finally drove her from her home by the time she was twelve. She was headed for a hard life on the streets of New Orleans. It was an edge that she skirted throughout her teens and it made her gun-shy of any relationship of any kind.

Family

The *Supreme Pilot* is from a very high-end, Washington, DC, family. Her father is the FBI director and her mother is a leading socialite who wants to marry her daughter off well. Just because the *Supreme Pilot* is her father's daughter, it doesn't spare her being blown about by the powerful whims of her highly-connected mother. She loves her family, she just doesn't know what to do with them: her father's habitual silence and her mother's constant matchmaking.

The *Latina Gunner* is the daughter of a coke whore and who knows—her mom sure doesn't. In addition to forcing both independence and self-reliance on her, it taught her to the very core that family was shit and anyone who said otherwise was snorting something far worse than coke.

The *Mechanic Next Door*'s mother died in childbirth and her father was reported to have burned to death in a helo crash when she was twelve. This drove her to best the "devil machine" that had killed her father. Her life is dedicated to making the helicopters better and safer and it is all she cares about—even knowing that someday one of these devil machines will kill her. It has forced her to seek perfection from herself in maintaining them and she will accept no less from others.

The *Wildcard Pilot*'s mother left when she was young and her father is a crooked cop. When her own safety becomes an issue, she runs away. Desperate, thinking to sell her body, she comes to the back door of a brothel. The aged madam adopts her and uses her in the kitchen and to clean the rooms but won't let her join the working girls. She learns that life is hard and all that can save you is an old woman and a sense of humor. She develops a real devil-may-care-but-I-sure-don't attitude.

Occupation

The *Supreme Pilot* is a West Point officer. The way she breaks into the Night Stalkers? She's so good that they can't keep her out. She is driven to lead her team to be the very best and to do it by setting the perfect example.

The *Latina Gunner* enlisted in the Army after her friend was gunned down because she figured they would feed her and it just might increase her life expectancy a little. She makes the Night Stalkers by being the best, most aggressive gunner there is.

The *Mechanic Next Door* was a natural for her occupation as a Black Hawk crew chief. With her photographic memory, she knows every system and how it interacts with every other system. She can make a helicopter hum like no one else. People—who don't come with blueprints and wiring diagrams—are utterly incomprehensible to her.

The *Wildcard Pilot* was on the verge of starting a prostitute's life when 9/11 changed her life. Suddenly the world was bigger than her little corner of New Orleans and she saw that flying to help her country just might be another option to a short, painful life on the streets.

Attitude

Some of this is touched on above, but it changed and morphed as they moved into their occupational roles. So I boiled it down to just a few choice words.

The *Supreme Pilot*: Meticulous. She'd no more make a mistake flying than she would in how she handled her personnel. Relationships? They are handled just as thoughtfully and carefully—and with just as little passion.

The *Latina Gunner*: Attack. It's her answer to everything: warfare, sex, arguments, and relationships. She'd never think to give an inch, including never letting anyone come close to her feelings.

The *Mechanic Next Door*: Precision. A painful introvert who has given everything she has in blind pursuit of perfection. She doesn't even know she has anything personal to give.

The *Wildcard Pilot*: Conflicted. One moment she's an absolutely awesome pilot and the next she's a total screw-up, pissing off her commander and unintentionally endangering others.

Summary

See how incredibly distinct these characters have become by combining looks, childhood, family, and occupation to form attitude?

There are two things I'd like to point out about how I used these tools.

First, these examples are all in the military romantic suspense genre. So they all have men who match them—though not necessarily in the way you'd expect. Each man has just as much development I could discuss, but here's the short form so you can see how this tool can be used to create tension.

The *Supreme Pilot*. Her counterpart is the sterling commander. He finds the best and then hones it to a razor's edge—perhaps even to the breaking point.

The *Latina Gunner*. The man she sweeps off his feet is pure upper-crust Boston and an exceptional pilot and strategist. She's very tactical, all about the moment; he's the calm master of the big picture.

The *Mechanic Next Door*. He's all about people. A master mechanic in his own right—the only sort of person the *Mechanic Next Door* could ever be with—he comes from a large family (she has none) and is everybody's pal (she can hardly speak around others).

The *Wildcard Pilot*. He's just as conflicted as she is. He was the black sheep of a very respectable family who he loves dearly. He was only saved from personal disaster by the same event she was: 9/11.

Second, how much of this did I know ahead of writing the books?

Their four photos.

Um…

Yeah, that's it.

I wrote these books blind. It was only as I started trying to analyze *how* I wrote such cool characters that I realized I was using this set of tools. It was only in retrospect that I understood that all my previous practice had instinctively led me to break down the elements I needed in order to understand and develop these characters into distinct individuals.

It took me longer to understand that this is *why* they are the way they are and *why* they respond the way they do. In the chapter after next, we'll look at *how* they respond. *How* they express themselves as characters. But first it's important to talk about a character's personal language.

4

Language

A CHARACTER'S language is often thought to be as simple as "Do they have an accent?"

First, I have a confession to make: I *suck* at talking with an accent. I've been told that my Scottish accent swings between Australian and Bulgarian. My fake French accents sound like anything but. And my Italian accents all sound like Brooklyn—bad, inaccurate, sloppy Brooklyn—that sometimes jumps to, you guessed it, Australia again. When it comes to me and accents? *Fuhgeddaboudit.*

What's worse is, I also suck at *writing* accents. Inverting sentence structures, slaughtering plurals, screwed-up word compounding… *Nope!* Not so much.

I won't say it's a blessing, but it isn't quite the crippling problem I'd thought it was when writing people from foreign places. It forced me to learn more about language than just an accent (which I really, really, *really* wish I had a facility with).

So, if like me, you have a tin ear for accents, or if you think that an accent is all that's necessary to make a character's language as distinct as it could be, read on.

Here are my thoughts about the five layers of a character's language. (This is true of a real, live person's as well.)

Side Note: Getting Started on Language

For me, the awareness of a structure behind a character's language started on a New York subway ride. While we'd talked often enough on the phone, I hadn't been back from the West Coast to see my sister in New York in years. So when she met a friend and me at the airport, we climbed aboard the subway and began catching up.

By sheer chance, my friend ended up between us.

The friend's comment after the long ride (during which they didn't say a word): "It's like being trapped in stereo Buchman."

I'd never thought about "Buchman" being a language before that moment. That started my journey of going deeper into a character than simply their country of origin.

Country

A country of origin isn't only about accent. It also doesn't have to be portrayed in mangled syntax. Sometimes it's enough to state what country they're from or allow them to speak the occasional key word under stress.

"Merci!" Jacquie said with a disdain that only a French woman could deliver properly while thanking someone. "Your help was neither requested nor required."

Even with a facility for language, an attitude is far easier and often more compelling to deliver.

She flicked a single, perfectly obsidian fingernail in an elegant gesture—that told me to go straight to hell and do something anatomically impossible.

The reason isn't that language or an accent aren't powerful—they are. But what's even more powerful is opinion. Because opinion is, by its very nature, filtered through character. So I make Jacquie more French by having my point-of-view character observe her inherent Frenchness. We've now reinforced it in several ways for the reader. A single word in French, the rest of the dialog is syntactically correct English—high-brow and snooty even. But in just two lines (three if you're compulsively counting periods), Jacquie is undeniably French. We can hear and see her to some extent and now.

We also learn about the narrating character. We're waiting for the next line to find out their reaction—amused, pissed, intrigued, embarrassed. A minor tension for the reader, but one that makes us curious to read the next line.

A country has mannerisms and customs, some of which can be found using online searches or by talking to people who would know. Some are simply handy cultural stereotypes. Let me point out that stereotypes typically exist for a reason—almost all have a basis in reality and can be used.

I traveled around the world by bicycle some years ago. I met more than my fair share of rude German tourists (who were flawlessly polite on home soil), crassly oblivious Americans, humble Japanese, and brash Australians, to name but a few.

If you're going to use a stereotype, do find a way to make it fresh, but it is a fine starting point to leverage their country-of-origin or country-of-choice language and mannerisms. The more you learn about a country, the easier this is to leverage. You can even leverage it backward.

Unlike most Americans, Pete's easy skill at engaging with people earned him the French woman's brilliant smile despite the finger she'd just given him.

Also, if you need to leverage a particular place, it's typically done more easily and clearly in narration than language.

"Merci!" Jacquie said with a disdain that only a Parisian fashionista, posed just so on the Pont des Arts bridge over the Seine, could deliver properly while thanking someone. "Your help was neither requested nor required."

One final comment on country: it's better to leave out a detail than get it wrong.

She flicked two fingers upward as if slapping my chin with a pair of perfectly obsidian fingernails in an elegant gesture—that told me to go straight to hell and do something anatomically impossible.

An incredibly rude gesture in the UK, in France it means that you want two of something and carries no connotations at all.

Did I know this? No. I did a quick search to make sure that the French actually use "the finger." They do, and it's *significantly* ruder to do so than it is in America. It's a good way to start a fight in France. Perhaps the way to show that, if it matters for your story, might be:

...that told me to go straight to hell and do something anatomically impossible in a manner so rude that my amusement was slapped aside and I shot her between those perfect breasts. I felt no remorse as I watched her body tumble backward over the rail to float down

the Seine with a final look of surprise pursed on those lovely lips for all eternity.

Or maybe not.

Region

Every country has regionalisms. If you know them, or can research them, go for it. Again, unless you are particularly skilled, spice is sufficient.

A Texan adores metaphors ("that alley was darker than a dog's butt"). A Mainer (often called a Mainiac) is notably laconic and loves nothing so much as baiting a tourist. A Californian often speaks without *any* emphasized consonants. City folk talk faster, rural ones slower. The Scottish love laying on a brogue until they're wholly incomprehensible to someone they want to mess with. (I had a freshman roommate in college who was something like seventeenth-generation American *and* pureblood redheaded Scot. He had no discernable accent until he started drinking. An' the drunker he got, te thikr hiz brogue wen' 'til ya kouldna unnerstan' a wor' 'e said.)

Regionalisms can be done with the tricks mentioned in Country above, but I find that works less well. If region truly matters in a country big enough to have clear accents, be sure to site them properly.

You sound like a Hamburger.

In German, the accent of residents of the city of Hamburg are considered to have the highest, most "true" German accent. It can either be a compliment or you can be telling a New Yorker, "You're just so Upper East Side," or a Londoner, "Oooo, aren't we ever-so posh?"

I think that getting a regionalism wrong is more likely to bump a reader out of a story than anything else to do with language. That said, the reverse is true: I don't think that anything can anchor a character more solidly than a good, proper regionalism. Or even a cliched one like this:

"Ma'am, you make me feel like a cat with nine tails at a rockin' chair convention. Yes, ma'am, you most certainly do."

Search the phrase "Dialect Quiz" online. *The New York Times* has both a US and a British-Irish dialect quiz that is utterly fascinating. In twenty-five words, it pinned down where I grew up during my language formation years within fifty miles even though I haven't lived anywhere near there since I was six (Lexington, Massachusetts, USA). I'm especially intrigued by the localization maps for each of the phrases, I use them often (warning, this quiz can also be a total rabbit hole—you'll need to create an account, but they don't appear to do anything with it).

Family / Team

Now it starts getting interesting. Remember "Stereo Buchman" from earlier?

Country and Region habits are primarily set by the age of ten, some would argue by the age of six. (Not being a linguist, I'll leave it at that.) Country and regional language are set by what we hear everywhere around us.

Family probably forms just as early, but it has a slightly different origin. It's what we hear at home or in the workplace. "Stereo Buchman" that I mentioned earlier comes from the fact that my mother was a huge reader of the classics and my father always wished he'd ended up as a college English professor rather than a computer engineer.

They were also both very Victorian England in their attitudes and literature. "Children are to be seen and not heard" was only the least of our house rules.

I spent many meals standing at the sideboard while my dinner got cold, reading from Webster's Unabridged Dictionary to settle some familial debate. Reading the key definition wasn't sufficient, of course. I also read pronunciations, word origins, and all definitions, concluding with common synonyms and antonyms. To say that I loved words would be so wrong. Little knowing how well this experience would serve me decades later when I started writing, those numerous hours (because one definition often led to another and another) are not fondly remembered.

However, that tenacious need to fully understand the nuances of every word *is* a part of my familial language. To this day, I can't leave an unknown word or slang alone and must look it up (though I typically stop after the short definition and word origin now).

Part of my familial language is an unlikely commonality of archaic British words and a penchant for polysyllabic articulations and convoluted sentence structures that are the bane of existence for my wife, family, and editor. (See, that sucker of a sentence is the way a part of me wants to write…I try to suppress it at every chance.) I must also confess that rather than creating a direct statement, expressing myself through a backhand negative would be my primary choice. (Yet I have used those precise tools to illuminate certain characters as well.)

Team language is so similar that I've included it under the same heading. It is a learned language, but from time spent together.

A team, when it coalesces and spends a long time on a project, gains a language of its own based on common experience. We often don't need to be told how these came about to see the bond that makes these people a team rather than a collection of characters.

"You're dumber'n Jasper's hound dog."

"Shee-it! Ain't nobody that stupid," Samuels joined in the laugh but vowed to get Vern back for that one. Besides, he'd liked that damned dog.

Which, of course, everyone on the team would know: both that he would get Vern back for that and that he'd always had a soft spot for that dog. It doesn't necessarily have to show the closeness of the bond, it merely shows its connectedness.

"You're dumber'n Jasper's hound dog."

Samuels punched him hard enough to bloody his nose and send him tumbling backward out of the helo's cargo bay door at ten thousand feet without a parachute. A good job finally done. Besides, he'd liked that damned dog, even if it hadn't been the sharpest critter on God's green Earth.

Occupation

In the workplace this may seem like a team language. But it goes beyond that.

I was a professional, certified project manager for a number of years. I could walk into a meeting with any of the half-million global members spread across the three hundred chapters of the Project Management Institute and we would understand each other (assuming they spoke English).

Why?

Because we were all trained to understand ROI,

schedule slack, black swan planning in risk mitigation, and a hundred other phrases. Had we shared a particular project, we'd also probably have an overlay of team language as described above.

This is true of every occupation.

In theater it might have been hotspots, stage right and left, spikes, dead spots (both light and sound), spill, teaser, and a hundred more. In the military, ROE—Rules of Engagement—tell a soldier what they are and aren't allowed to do when provoked in different ways.

Portfolio management is a completely different concept to a stockbroker, a project manager, and an artist.

But it goes beyond even that.

It isn't only a vocabulary that we share, it is a vocabulary that includes or excludes.

The military romances where the Special Ops hero rescues the civilian damsel in distress (and yes, there are still tons of those) and starts speaking about M4s, flash-bangs, and exfiltrations—*and she understands*—make me beyond crazy.

The Thomas Crown Affair has a great example of the right way to use this. A police detective specializing in hardcore, big-city crime is suddenly jacked into an art theft case. He spends almost the entire movie in over his head. However, the sexy insurance agent serves to educate him (and, conveniently, the audience as well) as they go along. She also recognizes the criminal early on because he speaks her language even if the detective doesn't.

I think that all of these elements, from country to occupational language, serve to make the character unique, but occupational language's power is in that inclusion / exclusion pairing.

Personal

This is the unique blend of all of the above.

This is the language that is uniquely mine (uh, cough cough, I mean the character's) and is slowly pieced together over the course of many pages of a story.

It must be consistent and it is, if I did my job right, unique.

Personally, I'm intense, I jump subjects with few cues, I'm well-educated but like the power of a curse word almost as well as I like the power of the precisely selected syllogism (If A and B are true, what the hell do we know about C?). I was a project manager in law, construction, tourism, and complex computer systems. I've sailed a fifty-foot boat solo, had a private airplane license for several years, and bicycled solo around the world. I'm an introvert who is very comfortable in a team player or leadership role but completely falls apart if I'm meeting a stranger. I'm a Jew who grew up all over New England but spent forty years in the Pacific Northwest.

All of this affects my language.

Would you use all of this if you were writing M. L. Buchman the character? Good Lord, no! For one thing, I'd sound like even more of a fool than that paragraph makes me appear. And for the other thing, you the writer would die trying to get all of those disparate pieces into anything short of an epic saga.

But there's immense depth there in that character that's me. By plucking out threads, we can have a character that speaks:

- Too much and too fast (or worse: too much and too slow).
- Terribly analytically or not.

- In artistic terms of colors and balance (we'll get into this later).
- From a place of reverence or lack of it.
- With an accent or not.
- And myriad others.

The combination of the five elements of language—country, region, family, team, and occupation—form the language of self.

On the Page

As we're discussing written language here, there's one more point to consider: How does that character's voice look on the page?

- Sentences are short and clipped, bare of anything except the necessities.

"You're wrong. We are about to crash." Josh folded his hands and awaited the inevitable.

- Sentences are short and clipped, but deeply cluttered with narrative thoughts and reactions.

"You're wrong," but Josh truly wished she wasn't. He'd only just started to really get to know the woman he'd flown with for three years and never touched until last night. And now their chances of survival were falling faster than the stock market on the first day of the Great Depression. Of course, sadly, throwing themselves out a skyscraper window wouldn't be any less effective than plummeting earthward in a broken space capsule. "We are about to crash."

- Chatty. Take that entire previous example and push it into run-on dialog.
- Furious. A lot of dialog, but all of it in short clipped sentences.
- Demonstrative. Run-on dialog with wild gesticulations and pounding of fists against inert consoles. (Which might fix things. Who knows?)

Again, we're limited by only the imagination. I use this tool quite a bit to distinguish my characters. It can be really fun.

I mentioned earlier what I did to the *Mechanic Next Door*. She speaks in short and clipped sentences that are always on point, but she's a deep thinker—making her dialogue light and narrative heavy. Her love interest is the natural storyteller and always glad of a laugh, however the only thing that he ever really thinks deeply about is the enigmatic woman he can't look away from—so he's dialogue heavy and narrative light. This makes the two characters, who are very different, also *look* very different on the page.

Four Night Stalker Women in Review

The Supreme Pilot

The Latina Gunner

The Mechanic Next Door

The Wildcard Pilot

So here they are again, let's look at them now that we've walked this whole path, including what I knew about them from the prior chapter.

The *Supreme Pilot*: Meticulous. She'd no more make a mistake flying than she would in how she handled her personnel. Relationships? They are handled just as thoughtfully and carefully—and with just as little passion. Her language is: Country/Region: DC elite. Family: minimally social, mostly keeping her own counsel like her father. Occupation: military officer. Personal: rock steady in any situation. Probably a little low on a sense of humor. Her thoughts rarely wander beyond the subject at hand.

The *Latina Gunner*: Attack. It's her answer to everything: warfare, sex, arguments, and relationships. She'd never think to give an inch, including never letting anyone come close to her feelings. Her language is: Country/region: Latina and East LA. Family: the effing street, man. Get a grip. Occupation: gunner fits her perfectly. Personal: fast, always on the move. Doesn't have much to say, but always says it with a cargo full of teasing slag mixed in with that shit.

The *Mechanic Next Door*: Precision. A painful introvert given everything she has in blind pursuit of perfection. She doesn't even know she has anything personal to give. Her language is: Country/Region: Fort Rucker, Alabama, but really the US Army. Family: again the US Army, reinforcing the country/region. Occupation: mechanic gives her a language of precision and double-checking everything. Personal: doesn't speak unless spoken to and only in short sentences about the topic at hand, but is a deep thinker with strong internal dialog.

The *Wildcard Pilot*: Conflicted. One moment she's an absolutely awesome pilot and the next she's a total screwup, pissing off her commander and unintentionally endangering others. Her language is: Country/Region: New Orleans, street, and slangy. Family: a crooked cop and a brothel madam give her a jaundiced view of everything. Occupation: a pilot of a thirty-million-dollar helicopter gives her a command authority that she's so not comfortable with. Personal: sass, without the gunner's biting edge, but nothing *but* sass so that she can hide who she really is— who she has no confidence in. And for a girl to give someone proper sass? That can take a whole bunch of words at times.

5

Viewing Their World

TWO CHAPTERS back I left you with a cliffhanger.

The idea that looks, childhood, family, and occupation combine to form attitude.

That this is *why* they are the way they are and *why* they respond the way they do.

Then we voyaged into personal language, which controls *what* language they speak.

The final question is *how* they perceive and respond. *How* they express themselves as characters.

This is based on their own senses and personality types in ways not covered above. I touched on this at the end of the prior chapter when I said that they might speak in artistic terms of colors and balance.

Side Note: NLP

I first learned about Neuro-Linguistic Programming, well…many years ago. It was in a class called Other Than Conscious Communication. I didn't get involved with either NLP or OTCC beyond that single weekend. I actually only remember one lesson from that, but it's the basis of this whole next discussion.

A Simple Test

Okay, before you do anything else, there's a word on the next page. I want you to note down the very first thing that comes to mind when you see the word. It's not a perfect illustration, but it will make the point. Remember, you must commit to your first reaction, not vacillate as I discuss it afterward. Write it down if you need to. Or repeat it a few times. Very first thing that comes to you.

Ready?

Here we go.

BELL

Okay, got your first reaction? Let's break it down a little.

- You *saw* a bell. Any kind of a bell.
- You *heard* a bell. A doorbell, a church bell, a school bell telling you that you're late for class as you hunker down in the locker you'd been stuffed in.
- You *felt* a bell. This is me. The first thing that comes to mind for me is the deep vibration in my gut from a big church bell. The second thing is the muffled shrillness of the school bell piercing my ears—while hunkered down in aforesaid locker.
- You wanted to *write* the word "bell."
- You *smelled* the bell. Seriously, you smelled the brass of a big bell or (again dating myself) the slightly acrid scent of burning insulation on a doorbell's transformer. Or even the smell of the locker you'd been stuffed into.

VAK Learning Styles Discussion

Here's a simple explanation of your results (remembering that this test is *drastically* oversimplified):

- *Visual:* You saw the bell. You are a visual learner. Illustrations are a great way for you to consume information. A professor who did demos or had slide decks just made your heart sing. Podcasts probably suck, but video podcasts are great.
- *Auditory:* You heard the bell. You are an auditory learner. Lectures are great. Pictures

don't help so much. Audio podcasts are awesome.

- *Kinesthetic:* You felt the bell. A pure kinesthetic finds no purpose in lectures and illustrations, but show them how to do it themselves once and they never forget.
- *Read/Write:* You wanted to write the word. You learn by putting pen to paper (or fingers to keyboard). This isn't very applicable in building fictional characters (except maybe an anal police detective with their little notebook) so I won't touch on it much again.
- *Olfactory:* You smelled the bell. These are the master chefs. Excellent food and smells aren't merely good or even lovely, they're orgasmic.

Now nobody is purely any one of these, and you *can* learn to use one(s) that aren't your primary learning mode(s)—somewhat.

Side Note: Where do you fit in compared to others?

There are percentages on how the population breaks down over these various styles of learning. And nobody agrees on what those percentages are. Some say that all are roughly equal except the fifth one—everyone agrees that a true Olfactory/Gustatory is exceedingly rare (<0.5% of people). Back when I learned this, they hadn't recognized the Read/Write mode yet. I find it better to ignore the numbers.

Personally, I'm *way* over in the corner of Kinesthetic. I learn hands-on. I became a better than average masseuse by two masseuses getting into an argument over the best way to give a massage and using my back as a demonstration tool. I've learned how to speak to visuals and auditories, but that was and is a lot of work.

My secondary learning mode is Read/Write (remember, no one is purely anything even though we'll talk about that later). By sitting in a class lecture, I learn almost nothing. But I get a degree of internal ownership when I take notes. I pretty much never have to read the notes again, but without that step, it's just so much *blah, blah, blah.* When I really need to learn something? I handwrite the notes in class, then I go home that night and type them up. Double Read/Write learning in two slightly different ways really anchors the material for me.

What on Earth does this have to do with character?

VAK Learning Styles Explained Another Way

Their learning style will drastically change how a character perceives their world and expresses themselves.

- A Visual will perceive and express through color and balance. They use phrases like: "I see what you mean." They will often, unconsciously, paint the picture of their words with their hands (typically hands up, palms out). If you hear that "So-and-so has lovely hands," it's often because they are visuals who are waving them about in graceful patterns as if painting their thoughts on a canvas as they speak them.
- An Auditory's hands will typically remain quiet by their sides. They're listening as if that's all that matters, because it is. "I hear what you're saying," is a common phrase. They will often

seem strangely passive, but they aren't missing a word.

- A Kinesthetic says, "I can feel that." From personal experience, I can tell you that's completely accurate. I literally "feel" when something is right or is off-kilter. We'll tend to speak with our palms up, but held low, as if we're holding something weighty (the truth, a brick, we have no idea what, but we're holding it).
- A Gustatory says, "That's got the right flavor," or something equivalent. They often tip their heads up as if sniffing after the truth.

If you want to learn more about this, just search online VAK Learning Styles (or even just VAK). I find the "images" results plenty useful. There's more there than you'll probably ever want to know.

And you repeat:

What on earth does this have to do with character?

Example

Let me introduce you to four other women from my contemporary romance series Where Dreams. These women I intentionally set out to use VAK Learning Styles differentiation. (Remember what I said earlier about practice. This is what I was practicing for this entire series.)

Four Where Dreams Women

The Food Critic   The Lawyer

The Fashion Designer   The Supermodel

The *Food Critic:* She's obviously my Gustatory. And her language will include words like: flavor, nuance, complement, etc.

The *Lawyer:* She's my Auditory as she makes her living by her words. Think polysyllabically precise lawyer-speak including discoverable, verifiable, and actionable facts. She's very analytical (which we'll get to next), then she judges.

The *Fashion Designer:* She's my Visual and talks in terms of color, balance, enhancement, connection, completion, etc.. She's also my sexy, flaky, messed-up genius.

The *Supermodel:* She's oddly my Kinesthetic. She loves the feel of fabric, the fit of clothes, and the power of the runway walk. She'll speak of precision, poise, energy, and so on.

These women, like the group before them, also have partners—eventually. These love interests have very different modes of communicating and expressing themselves, which leads to real challenges.

My Gustatory food critic reluctantly falls for the Visual fashion photographer.

My Auditory lawyer can't stay away from the Gustatory Italian chef.

My Visual fashion designer loses her heart to the Kinesthetic opera stage manager.

My Kinesthetic supermodel gets swept away by an Auditory novelist.

Application

As you can see, this is a very flexible tool. It offers us another way to further divide how our characters perceive and communicate in the world.

If you recall the *Supreme Pilot*, she was very serious, very driven. That's how she speaks and responds. Now let's drive that through the filter of being Kinesthetic. Perhaps that's at the core of why she's such a good pilot—she *feels* her helicopter in flight until she practically melds with the machine.

The *Latina Gunner* is an amazing Visual, as is the *Mechanic Next Door* who can see all the aircraft systems in her head. Finally, the *Wildcard Pilot* is conflicted because she's actually a Gustatory (she ends up in restaurants time after time in the novel) and a Kinesthetic—she feels her helicopter like a dance and it's reflected in how she flies, whereas the *Supreme Pilot* flies like an arrow, which is absolutely reflected in the women they are.

It is easy to see that VAK Learning Styles lets us see how a character:

- Perceives the world around them.
- Speaks or gives voice to the reactions that are driven from our earlier tools of: Looks, Childhood, Family, Occupation, and Attitude.
- VAK Learning Styles is another filter on language as well, controlling how they respond overlaid with the language divisions of: Country, Region, Family/Team, Occupation, and Personal.

6

Oh, no! More tools

HERE ARE a couple of other major tools that I've seen used.

The Four Forces

Imagine, if you will, four boxes like this:

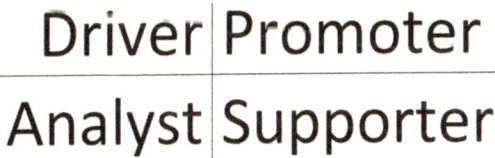

Driver	Promoter
Analyst	Supporter

These are four very distinct personality types.

- The *Driver* (aka the *Motivator*): Never satisfied, they're always pushing ahead. This is the one who rallies the troops for one more try. ("And I'll shoot you myself if you don't give it your all.")
- The *Promoter* (aka the *Rainmaker*): This highly-motivated extrovert thrives on the art of the

deal. On making it happen. The fact that it is completely impossible never enters into their consideration, or even their imagination. They believe that anything they think up, the rest of the folks can figure out how to do.

- The *Analyst* (aka the *Thinker*): This task-oriented introvert always gets stuck with being the one who has to figure out how to achieve what the *Promoter* promised on the *Driver's* timeline.
- The *Supporter* (aka the *Peacemaker*): This relationship builder really just wants everyone to get along.

There are numerous examples of this. One of my personal favorites is from *The Hitchhiker's Guide to the Galaxy*.

- The *Driver*: Trillian, the Earth girl who escapes to space before the Earth is destroyed, always wants to push ahead, find the next thing, perhaps because it's better than having to ever face herself.
- The *Promoter*: Zaphod Beeblebrox, the total space case and President of the Galaxy, is the font of wild ideas. He never cares about what's possible as long as they Go! Go! Go!
- The *Analyst*: Arthur, the Earthling who hopes they survive long enough to find a good cup of tea, does what all analysts do best: they worry and argue that everything is impossible until forced forward step by reluctant step.
- The *Supporter*: Ford, the researcher for *The Hitchhiker's Guide to the Galaxy* who accidentally got marooned on Earth and befriended Arthur, just wants everyone to have a good time.

Side Note: Unbalanced Forces

My first corporate job was as a paralegal and computer nerd for a law firm with four business partners. They, curiously, were the four forces embodied right out to the limits of stereotype.

The Driver was the top courtroom lawyer, the Promoter was awesome at getting clients (and The Truth was a very fuzzy concept during those pitches), the Analyst worried about all the details, and the Supporter made sure everyone was happy. This was a stable operation for years.

Then the Supporter got the offer he couldn't refuse: as a corporate in-house lawyer for his favorite client, which included more money and getting home to his family at a regular hour.

Within the year the firm had shredded itself. No one could control the Driver and it made the Analyst beyond crazy. With no practical controls on him, the Promoter started promoting things that the firm couldn't deliver at all.

Four Forces Example

Let's meet our four Where Dreams women again under different circumstances.

The *Food Critic:* Our Gustatory queen is also the group's *Driver.* She's always pushing ahead. She's so driven by career that she doesn't even see the relationship that she's stumbling into.

The *Lawyer:* Our Auditory lady is also our *Analyst.* She moves so slowly, so carefully, that she can't even see the relationship forming in front of her because it's happening so fast.

The *Fashion Designer:* The Visual, flaky genius is the group's *Supporter.* She has so much love in her heart for her friends that all she cares about is their happiness. In fact, she so focused on *their* happiness that she almost misses a chance at her own.

The *Supermodel:* Finally, our Kinesthetic supermodel is also the business genius *Promoter.* Everything she touches seems to turn to gold. On the personal side, not so much. Relationships are run like business deals, starting hot and ending fast—until she runs head-on into one that doesn't.

This creates unique problems for each character. Again, not to repeat myself too many times but…the more unique and distinct you can make your characters, the more deeply engaged your reader will be.

Myers-Briggs

This is the keystone of all personality tests. It's the monster in the playing field. Corporations deploy this test to applicants to see how they'll fit on the team. Average everyday people, who are otherwise rational in most ways, will make first date conversation like, "I'm an INTJ. Let me guess. Are you an INFP?"

If you haven't heard of this beast, go ahead and search for it online. I'm only going to spend a few lines on it.

A Myers-Briggs Type Indicator is four letters long and each position can be one of two things. This means that there are sixteen possible personality type combinations with reams published about the meaning of each one.

Here are the four variables (some of which mean far more than their simple keywords):

- Extraversion vs. Introversion
- Sensing vs. Intuition
- Thinking vs. Feeling
- Judging vs. Perceiving

I know authors who run each of their characters through a version of this test and then look up whether they're a compatible love interest, a good friend, an enemy, or a nemesis for the hero.

I've tried it and I found this to be far too cumbersome for my methods, but others swear by it.

Other Tools

There are numerous other tools out there. But the ones that I've included here are enough to keep me busy for a lifetime of characters. Even after more than sixty novels and seventy short stories, I feel as if I've barely scraped the surface.

Got a hot one? I'd love to see it at characters@mlbuchman.com.

7

Creating Memorable
Characters

SO FAR, we've only talked about creating *distinct* characters. Now I'd like to spend just a moment discussing how to create *memorable* ones.

What do I mean by a memorable character? It is the one particular character that so grabs a fan's attention that they will read every book with which that character is even lightly associated.

I've managed to do this once or twice (Emily Beale and Michael Gibson). How did I do it? I wish I knew.

But here is my current thinking on this topic.

Memorable Characters

First let's talk about some of the most memorable characters in fiction so that we agree what I'm talking about. In general, because the author hit on something that sold (or they enjoyed so much they couldn't stop writing about them), these characters appear in series. Below is just a tiny list; both you and I can think of tons more, but I just want to get the idea down.

- Sherlock Holmes by Arthur Conan Doyle
- Hercule Poirot by Agatha Christie
- Doc Savage by "Kenneth Robeson" (a house name that was mostly Lester Dent)
- James Bond by Ian Fleming
- Dirk Pitt by Clive Cussler (Curiously, Cussler was seeking to invent a new character and he decided to take half Doc Savage and half James Bond to create Pitt. Clearly, his plan worked.)
- Eve Dallas by J. D. Robb (Nora Roberts)
- Stephanie Plum by Janet Evanovich
- Jack Reacher by Lee Child
- Harry Potter, Ron Weasley, and Hermione Granger by J. K. Rowling
- Armand Gamache by Louise Penny (I haven't read these yet, so I won't discuss them, but it seems that everyone around me has, so he is fast ascending my to-read-soon list.)
- Anne (of Green Gables) Shirley by L. M. Montgomery
- Gandalf by J. R. R. Tolkien
- Emily Beale by M. L. Buchman (I've added my greatest success to date for discussion purposes. The *Supreme Pilot* fits the pattern, if not the fame of these other examples. Emily has launched dozens of novels and numerous short stories.)

A memorable character can absolutely exist in a single title as well. HAL, Elizabeth Bennet, Hannibal Lecter, Ahab and Moby Dick, Dirk Struan from *Tai-Pan*…again the list is wide and varied

Now that we agree on what a memorable character is, let's look a bit at how they got that way.

Side Note: Romancing the Series

A memorable series character can be extremely difficult in the romance context of any genre.

Why? Because once they find their true love, their story is "over" in many ways. It takes a master of the craft like Nora Roberts or Janet Evanovich to sustain a love story across multiple books (59 for Eve Dallas and 25 for Stephanie Plum respectively as of this writing). These romances are actually mysteries and sold that way, but romance readers do cross over and follow these extended love stories with great interest.

So what to do? This is why I included my Emily Beale in the list above. Her romance was complete and "done" by the end of Book One, The Night Is Mine. *However, I loved this character and worked to keep her in the future books. She took on the mentor / mother role to future couples and we had a lot of fun together.*

When it came time for her to retire from The Night Stalkers military romance series, she was far from done. She flew front and center through five novels of the Firehawks series, mentoring new couples in the world of heli-borne wildland firefighters.

She also insisted on guest appearances in her old world and finally retired in the Henderson's Ranch series, where she played a key role in eight more titles and helped launch another new series (though from mostly behind the scenes), the White House Protection Force.

By playing to her character strengths, she found a strong secondary role in over thirty titles. And even when the role is minor, books that include her significantly outsell anything else I write, marking her as a clear fan favorite.

Zuckerman's Basics Reconsidered

Again, his book *Writing the Blockbuster Novel* is definitely worth the read.

Here's his list of key elements again:

- High stakes for the character
- Larger-than-life characters
- Powerful dramatic question
- High concept
- Multiple POVs (almost always)
- Setting
- Family

He was writing about creating blockbuster novels (obviously by the title). But I find it interesting to apply this same criteria to creating a blockbuster (or at least memorable) character.

High stakes for the character: Imagine a hero who happens to rescue someone versus a hero who risks their life to rescue someone. We can *feel* (at least I call it that, being kinesthetic) the increased tension in the second half of that sentence. But is death the highest price to pay?

How about cornering your heroine to where she must decide whether to betray a loved one or herself? Ramp it up more: she must go against a core belief to save a loved one...even though they were wrong and crossed the heroine's internal moral line. Now we have betrayal by the loved one (especially if they did it knowingly) and betrayal of self.

The higher the character's personal stakes, the more vested we become in them. Dirk Pitt merely risks life and limb, as does James Bond. But Sherlock Holmes risks his very sanity if he can't solve a case. Elizabeth Bennet's pride unravels every belief and every heartfelt rule of society she's ever held dear, until she is finally able to shed it all at the very end. To up the stakes even more, Jane Austen has her do so only after she believes it is too late and she has destroyed her personal future forever and will die loveless and alone.

Larger-than-life characters: The memorable character is not just the local lawyer—unless he is Mitch McDeere in John Grisham's *The Firm,* who takes down an entire corrupt team of mafia lawyers at the risk of his marriage and his life.

The larger-than-lifeness of a character, their very exceptionality, is what draws us to them. As John Travolta once said, "You don't have to love the character, you have to want to watch them." Hercule Poirot is a pompous, effete Belgian—who is also the greatest detective to ever live and can solve cases that mystify the reader in surprising ways.

Every one of the characters above meet these criteria: Moby Dick (the greatest whale ever, who is also albino to boot), HAL (the lethally self-aware computer), Anne Shirley (the sunshine on the otherwise pragmatic Green Gables), Emily Beale (the first woman of The Night Stalkers), Harry Potter (the boy who lived), and so on and so on.

Powerful dramatic question: Here Zuckerman speaks about the story's dramatic question, but I find it useful to think about the character's dramatic question as well.

James Bond is asked to save Britain and Dirk Pitt is typically asked to save the world. Hercule Poirot and Sherlock live to solve the mystery.

But my favorite characters have more complex dramatic questions.

Gandalf: Can I be wise enough and powerful enough to save all of Middle Earth from the darkness of Sauron?

Mitch McDeere: Am I willing to trade my integrity to achieve my dreams?

Anne Shirley: Can an orphan find happiness? Do they even deserve it?

Harry Potter: Can I ever be more than who I think I am? Can I survive others' perceptions and expectations of me, both good and bad?

High concept: A story's high concept can be thought of as the simplest form to describe the tale. What is the character's high concept?

Ahab – a man to whom revenge is more important than life itself.

Jack Reacher – a loner who willingly lives outside the law but serves justice from an unstoppable moral code.

Or even Hannibal Lecter – he asks us if pure evil exists, can we live with it?

Multiple POVs (almost always): Multiple points of view is one of the most powerful tools available to a writer for establishing a memorable character. Why? I think this is two-fold:

- It allows us to step outside the character and see things that we couldn't otherwise know.
- It allows us to see how others see the main character.

Would Sherlock appear so brilliant, or have that tinge of vulnerability, if Dr. Watson didn't see it for us?

What purpose does Monsieur Bouc (the owner of the railway) serve in *Murder On the Orient Express* except to repeatedly tell us that Hercule Poirot is the greatest detective of all time?

Without Al Giordino constantly telling us, "There's no way we can survive if we try that!" would we find Dirk Pitt's achievements even half so impressive?

A multiple POV isn't always used, of course. Elizabeth Bennet sees Mr. Darcy as an arrogant, conceited, prideful...jerk. The impact when he transforms in her eyes to a thoughtful, caring, and shy man is enormous. But it *is* enhanced by the closest we ever come to seeing his own point of view of himself when he corrects her perceptions and his own bias through the one letter that he writes to her.

Setting: Name a single one of these characters that doesn't live in an amazing setting.

Dirk Pitt lives in a secret and secure airplane hangar with a luxury apartment upstairs and a stunning array of classic cars downstairs, but his adventures includes exotic global locales—mostly on or under water.

James Bond goes to the most exotic luxury settings.

Elizabeth Bennet lives in a crowded home so thick with family that she couldn't be anywhere else.

Emily Beale comes to life in the pilot's seat of a thirty-million-dollar Black Hawk helicopter.

Moby Dick is the king of the seven seas.

HAL actually *is* a spaceship.

Gandalf lives in Middle Earth.

Even Mitch McDeere, a man born into and struggling out of poverty, is suddenly in the lap of Southern luxury.

Setting defines and transforms character to make them more memorable.

Family: And family? It's hard to know where to begin. Family doesn't have to be blood relatives. In fact, it often isn't.

For Elizabeth Bennet it certainly is.

But James Bond, before he must confront the past at Skyfall, never faces his blood past. However, he still has a very real family. It's made up of the mother/father M, the brothers Q and Felix, and the sisterly (mostly) Moneypenny to tease.

Dirk Pitt has his "twin brother" sidekick Al, his

boss/father Admiral Sandecker, and his assistant "younger brother" Rudi. He eventually gets a wife along the way.

Family shows us their character and their weaknesses. It gives us background to measure their achievements against. Anne Shirley's measure in Green Gables is two-fold in family, both that she's an orphan and has no family, and the purest joy with which she creates a family of her own through sheer willpower.

Upping the Narrative

These elements from Al Zuckerman's book don't neces-sarily change how a character speaks, but they make the character much richer and much more distinct. By delving into the character's world through higher stakes and all the rest of it, we are creating a richer character—a more distinct and unique character.

Combining Zuckerman's criteria with the distinctive-ness achieved using language, VAK, the Four Forces diagram and others, we can create powerful and far more memorable characters. And, if we do it right and are very lucky, then our fans will want to follow them for a long time.

8

A Few Final Thoughts

Planning vs. Discovery

I TALKED EARLIER about Plotter versus Pantser, but I think it is worthwhile to circle back to these apparently disparate methodologies. Whether you start with a massive character profile or with the blank page and discover your character as you write, you are going to go through a similar process of developing your characters.

There's an inspirational seed: a picture, a gesture, the house they live in, a gait.

At first, you may not even know what they look like (unless you started with a picture) or how they move (unless you started with that). With time, you do.

Then you layer in odd facts: The only thing to distract them from a fine meal is a fine murder (Poirot). They do their best thinking while playing a violin (Sherlock). They want their martini shaken, not stirred (Bond).

You layer in more and more until you have your character. Then, as you start or continue writing, you discover more about the character in that process. Just like a book, a character is built in drafts. Whether the first draft is a character study or in the course of drafting a novel, it's still a first draft of a character.

I find this so useful a thought that I'm going to repeat it:

Just like a book, a character is built in drafts.

Thinking that your first iteration of a character is the complete character will give you a drunkard secret agent and a violin-playing detective. Whatever your creative process, understanding and using tools (like the ones in this book) will let you add as much richness to your character as you do to your story.

Do *not* neglect one for the sake of the other.

Precasting

I've written novels from intense preplanned characterizations and from barely conceived openings. Personally, I *love* the discovery aspect of the writing process. I love writing into the unknown and getting wrapped up in the story and the character.

But…

I'm going to suggest that precasting your character will probably strengthen your story more than any other action you can take. Precasting them, by knowing something of who and what they are *before* you plunge into the story, will help them be more distinct, more memorable. By having a clear(ish) vision of a character before I begin writing, I find that they interact with the story in their own, unique way far more strongly than if they are built along with the plot.

If you're a hard-and-confirmed pantser, I would ask you this: Are you restricting yourself by committing wholly to a particular process?

I ask this because I know that, for years, I was.

Now I precast all my main characters to some degree before I start writing. However, I also remain open to learning far more about them as I write the story and letting them change and grow.

Are you a hard-and-confirmed plotter? If so, I ask this: Do you so restrict your character to your original plan that they became inauthentic and you reject what you learn in the writing process?

I ask because I've done that too.

Think about what defines your comfort zone about character development…then nudge it and see what happens. It's just practice for the next book after all.

The Memorable Character

Unless you're a superfan, I dare you to tell me the plot based on a randomly selected title in a series. *But* if I say Jack Reacher, Stephanie Plum, Gandalf or Bilbo, HAL, Spock, or any others, you're going to know instantly what I'm talking about.

I don't care what genre you're in: *character trumps everything.*

Again, repeating myself:

Character trumps everything.

A lame character will not recover the most fantastic science fiction setting. An uninspiring one will no more drive a masterfully-plotted thriller than a piece of toast would. (Okay, I can hear someone out there deciding to write a piece-of-toast thriller. Do it up!)

Am I saying that the character needs to be at the forefront? No. A science fiction book, without a great setting also, can't be saved by any except the most amazing character. A thriller that has no fast-driven plot isn't so thrilling. But without a strong character, neither will amount to much. Picture *Moby Dick* without Moby and Ahab, *2001: A Space Odyssey* without HAL, or a terrifying serial killer loose in Washington, DC, without Alex Cross.

Character Thinking in a Series World

This book was born from a talk I entitled with that simple phrase. I was writing two series and had to start thinking about how to make my characters distinct. They were romances. The Night Stalkers was to be four books, slowly building a single military team. (That the world became over thirty-five novels and fifty short stories is just good fortune). The Where Dreams series was a trilogy of three friends reuniting in Seattle after ten years apart.

Side Note: Flexibility (an example)

The Where Dreams trilogy did indeed begin as a story of three college friends who finally all live in the same city a decade out of school. They've pursued distinct and separate lives and are now rediscovering their friendship, pursuing their careers, and (these are romances) finding their one true love.

However, two of the background characters that I created in the process were so distinct and so strong that it turned into a five-book series.

And three deeper background characters stepped up and called for their own short story romances. In total, three novels became five novels and three short stories just because of how distinct and unique the characters were.

The original three characters were the *Food Critic*, the *Lawyer*, and the *Fashion Designer*. I started out to write the first one about the *Food Critic*. It eventually became clear that my strongest character was the *Fashion Designer*, Perrin.

I considered pulling her book into the first place, but I was already so deeply into the book that I didn't change it.

Then for Book Two, I thought about the characters and decided to push Perrin to Book Three (which an unexpected Christmas novella actually made into Book Four). The reason I didn't write Perrin next was that I knew the strength of her character was going to pull readers right through my entire series out to (now) Book Four. I *intentionally* delayed the use of my strongest character for purposes of reader engagement.

The *Supermodel*, who became Book Five, had been quietly growing stronger without my noticing through all four books until she was so strong and so important that I had to give her a book as well. Perrin *started* strong and I used her strategically as I thought about the series. Melanie the *Supermodel* simply was so strong that she became the next logical step.

I made a similar choice in The Night Stalkers series, but it was far more conscious. When I completed the first book, *The Night Is Mine,* I knew that I had created not one, but two truly powerful and memorable characters: Emily Beale (the *Supreme Pilot*), and Michael Gibson (*Delta Force's greatest warrior*). I already had a four-book contract and I already knew what characters I wanted to include in those books.

My editor begged me to make Michael's story next, but I knew two things. I knew how strong he was and I knew that I wanted to sell more books to my editor and my fans. Therefore, I stuck to my guns and placed Michael as sixth in the series. Michael's true fans read through, waiting for (begging for) his story.

If this had been a thriller, my actions might not have looked much different.

A common technique when there is a team around a

central hero is to occasionally focus a story more strongly on one team member or another. One time our main hero is out on the edge with the chief sidekick (and we learn more about that team member), another time with the team's nerd. But what if it's the team's strong man who ends up, for whatever reason, being the next most intriguing character after the hero? You can delay the strong man's step to the fore until deeper in the series.

It's just a thought.

A Final Reminder

Do *not* try to build a character with all of these tools at once. Rationally, I'd suggest that you chose one tool, say "family" perhaps, and work with that for an entire story (or several, as family is a big one). Then try something else.

However, if you really want to try something masochistic, consider creating an amended interview (remember that first tool I mentioned) that each character must answer. Perhaps it is a Character Training Course, M. L's patented CT Course for Character Building. (Not really patented, but it sounds cool, right?)

- First: What do you look like? How do you move?
- Second: Let's talk about your childhood, family, occupation, and finally attitude.
- Third: What's your language? By country, region, family, team/occupation, and personal as a final form.
- Fourth: How do you perceive the world and how do you express yourself? VAK Learning Styles, Driver-Promoter-Analyst-Supporter, or even Myers Briggs.

- Fifth: What makes you memorable? High stakes, larger-than-life, powerful dramatic question, high concept, multiple POVs, setting, and family.

But that's a crazy idea.

I'd love to hear from you. Post a review and send me a link, or contact me directly via e-mail at characters@mlbuchman.com.

About the Author

M.L. Buchman started the first of over 60 novels, 70 short stories, and a fast-growing pile of audiobooks while flying from South Korea to ride his bicycle across the Australian Outback. Part of a solo around the world trip that ultimately launched his writing career.

All three of his military romantic suspense series—The Night Stalkers, Firehawks, and Delta Force—have had a title named "Top 10 Romance of the Year" by the American Library Association's *Booklist*. NPR and Barnes & Noble have named other titles "Top 5 Romance of the Year." In 2016 he was a finalist for Romance Writers of America prestigious RITA award. He also writes: contemporary romance, thrillers, and fantasy.

Past lives include: years as a project manager, rebuilding and single-handing a fifty-foot sailboat, both flying and jumping out of airplanes, and he has designed and built two houses. He now makes his living as a full-time writer on the Oregon Coast with his beloved wife and is constantly amazed at what you can do with a degree in Geophysics. You may keep up with his writing and receive a free starter e-library by subscribing to his newsletter at: www.mlbuchman.com

Other works by M. L. Buchman:

Short Story Series by M. L. Buchman:

The Night Stalkers
The Night Stalkers
The Night Stalkers 5E
The Night Stalkers CSAR
The Night Stalkers Wedding Stories

Firehawks
The Firehawks Lookouts
The Firehawks Hotshots
The Firebirds

Delta Force
Delta Force Short Stories

US Coast Guard
US Coast Guard

White House Protection Force
White House Protection Force Short Stories

Where Dreams
Where Dreams Short Stories

Eagle Cove
Eagle Cove Short Story

Henderson's Ranch
Henderson's Ranch Short Stories

Dead Chef Thrillers
Dead Chef Short Stories

Deities Anonymous
Deities Anonymouse Short Stories

SF/F Titles
The Future Night Stalkers
Single Titles

www.ingramcontent.com/pod-product-compliance
Lightning Source LLC
Chambersburg PA
CBHW031131020426
42333CB00012B/329